Crafts from Felt

by Huguette Kirby

Translated by
Cheryl L. Smith

Reading Consultant:
Dr. Robert Miller
Professor of Special Education
Minnesota State University, Mankato

Bridgestone Books

an imprint of Capstone Press
Mankato, Minnesota

Table of contents

words to know

assemble (uh-SEM-buhl)—to put parts of something together

cotton batting (KOT-uhn BAT-ing)—a layer or sheet of raw cotton used for lining quilts or stuffing craft items

embroidery thread (im-BROI-duh-ree THRED)—string used to sew designs on cloth

fray (FRAY)—to separate into single loose threads, especially at the edges of cloth; felt is good for crafts because it does not fray.

mobile (MOH-beel)—a sculpture made of several items balanced at different heights and hung from a central object

sachet (sa-SHAY)—a small, scented bag used to make clothes smell good

---

Originally published as *Feutrine*, © 1999 Editions Milan

Bridgestone Books are published by Capstone Press
151 Good Counsel Drive, P.O. Box 669, Mankato, Minnesota 56002
http://www.capstone-press.com

Library of Congress Cataloging-in-Publication Data
Kirby, Huguette.
Crafts from felt/by Huguette Kirby; translated by Cheryl L. Smith.
    p. cm.—(Step by step)
    Includes index.
    Summary: Provides step-by-step instructions and patterns for making twelve crafts from felt and thread, glue, beads, or other ordinary objects.
    ISBN 0-7368-1474-4 (hardcover)
    1. Felt work—Juvenile literature. [1. Felt work. 2. Handicraft.]
    I. Title. II. Step by step (Mankato, Minn.)
TT880 .K567 2003
746'.0463—dc21

                   2002000061

Editor:
Rebecca Glaser

Photographs:
Milan/Dominique Chauvet;
Capstone Press/Gary Sundermeyer

Graphic Design:
Sarbacane

Design Production:
Steve Christensen

1 2 3 4 5 6 07 06 05 04 03 02

Some Secrets about Felt

This book is about making crafts with colored felt. All you need is felt, glue, embroidery thread, and beads. You can make cats and dogs who get along well together, butterflies for your hair, fish to catch, and other fun objects. Decorate them for yourself or make gifts for other people. Follow the steps closely. You also can invent your own felt crafts.

Friendly Advice

→ Felt is a thick cloth that is simple to use. You can easily cut it and it does not fray, so you do not have to make hems. You can glue it, sew it, and paint it.

→ Use tacky glue to put together your felt projects. It is easy to use and holds well after it is dry. Tacky glue is available at craft stores.

→ For the more difficult shapes, use the patterns on pages 30–31.

How to Stamp Felt

1 Make your designs on the felt with very thick paint.

2 Cover your design with a sheet of paper and press it with your hand to flatten the paint. Then remove the paper.

4

Materials

You will need these materials in addition to the ones listed with each activity.

felt

scissors

paper

glue stick

tacky glue

embroidery thread

paint brush

paint

USE WITH ADULT HELP:

utility knife

embroidery needle

wire

5

Picture cards

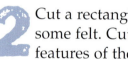

1 Glue the colored paper to the card stock with the glue stick.

2 Cut a rectangle out of some felt. Cut out features of the face.

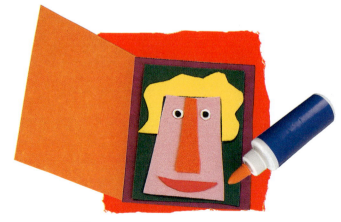

3 Use tacky glue to glue the felt rectangle to the card. Then glue the face pieces on top.

You can get ideas for your picture cards by looking at paintings by famous artists. Pablo Picasso used simple shapes to paint pictures of objects, people, and landscapes.

Let's Fish

3 Using a pencil, stuff your fish with cotton batting. Be careful not to poke the pencil through the side. Do not overstuff the fish.

1 Cut two fish shapes of the same size. Then cut eyes, mouth, stripes, and fins.

2 Glue the details on both fish. Glue the two shapes together. Leave an opening at the top. Let the glue dry for one hour.

4 Open a paper clip and put it in the opening. Glue the fish closed. Make a fishing pole with the dowel and a piece of wire.

8

Make a fishing game by hanging your fish from a closet rod with string. Push all the fish to get them moving. Then see how many you can catch on your pole.

Space Mobile

You Will Need:
- **Wire**
- **Tacky glue**
- **Branch**
- **Paint**

1 Glue a wire between two squares of felt. Make many squares. Let them dry for 15 minutes.

2 Cut out planets, stars, and rockets from the squares. Do not cut through the wire.

3 Find a dead branch and paint it. When it has dried completely, hang your shapes on it using the pieces of wire.

10

Constellations are groups of stars in the sky. A star chart shows a map of constellations. Check a star chart and make your mobile look like a constellation.

Butterflies

3 Cut out different shapes of felt and glue them to the wings.

1 Glue together two felt rectangles of different colors. Let them dry for 15 minutes.

4 Have an adult make two antennas out of wire and beads. Cut out a small rectangle of felt and cover it with glue. Place the antennas on the felt and tightly roll the felt around them to make the body.

2 Cut out the shape of a butterfly from the rectangles.

5 Glue the body to the wings. Make more butterflies with different shapes and colors. Glue the butterflies on a headband, barrettes, or pins.

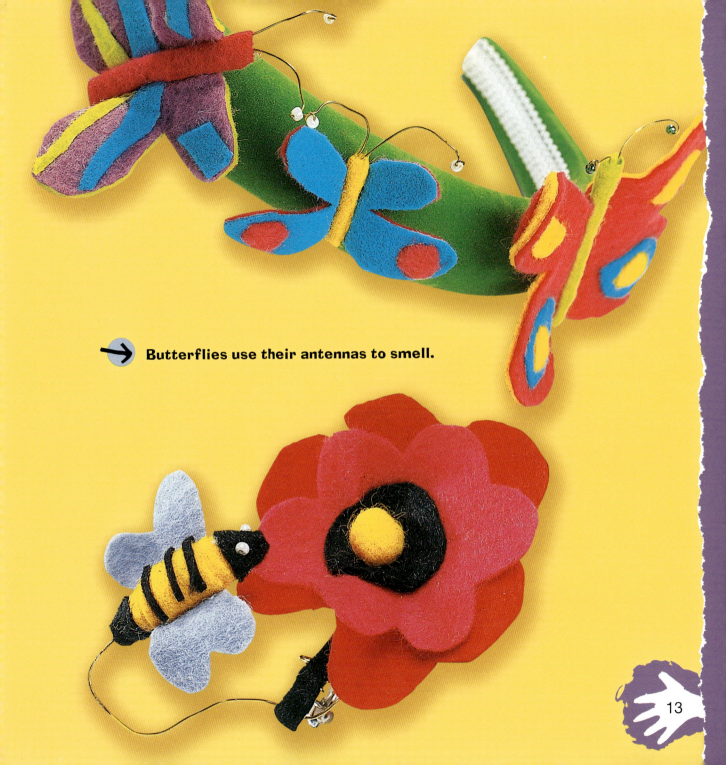

Butterflies use their antennas to smell.

13

Pencil Holder

You Will Need:
- **Potato chip can**
- **Sheet of tagboard**
- **Pencil**
- **Tacky glue**

2 With the scissors, cut out the shape.

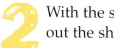

1 Ask an adult to cut off the top of the potato chip can so it is shorter. Place it on the tagboard. Trace a circle around it and then draw the shape of grass.

4 Cover the can with a piece of felt. Glue the can to the tag board. Fold the grass to the front of the can. Glue the flower to the stem. Then glue the stem to the back of the can.

3 Glue the shape to a piece of felt. Let it dry for one hour. Then cut around the shape. Cut out a flower and stem from the tagboard. Glue each shape to a different color felt.

Felt is made by heating wool with water and chemicals. The wool fibers then are pressed together to make cloth.

15

Frightening Finger Puppets

1 Follow the pattern on page 31 to cut two head shapes. Then cut the other details for the face.

2 Glue the hair and the ears to the head. Put glue around the edges of the other piece except at the bottom.

3 Assemble the two pieces. Then glue the features to the face. Let it dry for one hour.

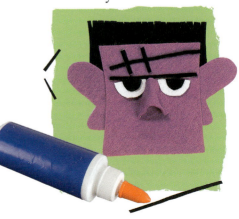

16

Make a Halloween puppet show with these finger puppets. Did you know that people once wore costumes to scare away evil spirits on Halloween?

House Key chains

You Will Need:
- **Key rings**
- **Tacky glue**
- **Cotton batting**
- **Pencil**

3 Let the house dry for one hour. Then stuff it with cotton batting by using a pencil.

1 Cut out two pieces of felt for the house. Cut other pieces for the windows, door, and other details. Put a small strip of felt around the key ring to make a handle.

2 Glue the details on one of the two houses. Then put glue around the edges of the other house. Leave the top side open. Assemble the two houses.

4 Put the strip of felt with the key ring between the houses. Close the rest of the opening with glue.

18

In about 1750, a person in Great Britain invented a glue made from fish.

19

Sachets

You Will Need:

- **Embroidery thread and needle**
- **Scented items (spices or flower petals)**
- **Beads**
- **Tacky glue**

1 Cut two squares of felt about 4 inches (10 centimeters) on each side. Next, cut four small squares about 1 inch (2.5 centimeters) wide, and four smaller circles.

2 Assemble the two large squares by sewing them together on three sides. Fill the sachet with the scented items, then sew the last side.

3 Sew together a small felt square, a felt circle, and a bead. Repeat this for the other three squares. Make a knot on top of each bead and cut the thread.

4 Glue the four small squares on the sachet.

20

You can leave the scents out and use the same felt design to make pillows, place mats, or picture frames.

Flat vases

1 Stamp a piece of felt, following the directions on page 4. Let the paint dry.

3 Then cut off the felt around the edge of the cardboard.

2 Cut out the shape of a vase from the cardboard. Glue it to the back of the felt piece. Let it dry for one hour.

4 Glue the glass jar to the back of the vase. Let it dry for one day before putting flowers in it.

22

Cut flower stems at an angle underwater to make the flowers last longer. The stems can soak up more water if you cut them this way. Be careful not to get the cardboard wet when you pour water into the jar.

23

TWO-SIDED PUPPETS

1 Trace the shape of the puppet on page 30 onto the felt. Cut it out.

2 Put glue around the edges, except for the bottom. Glue this shape onto a larger felt rectangle.

3 Allow the puppet shape to dry for one hour. Then cut around the shape of the puppet.

4 Cut a blouse and a skirt shape from different colors of felt. Sew thread through the top of the skirt to make a ruffle.

5 Glue the blouse and skirt to the puppet. Add other objects like ribbons, beads, or yarn to make the details of the face and clothes.

→ **You can make two people on one puppet. Put different features on the front and back. Then turn your hand around and the prince becomes a frog.**

Tabletop Puppet Stage

You Will Need:
- **Cardboard box**
- **Paint**
- **Large piece of cardboard**
- **Tacky glue**

1 Find a cardboard box and ask an adult to cut out the bottom for you. Paint the rest of the box black.

2 On a different large piece of cardboard, trace the shape of a TV. Ask an adult to cut out the screen for you.

3 Glue the screen onto some felt. Trim around the inside and outside edges.

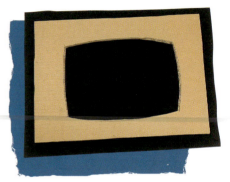

4 Glue colored pieces of felt around the TV. Now glue the screen to the box.

In Asian countries such as Indonesia and Vietnam, people put on plays with shadow puppets. Turn your puppets into shadow puppets by hanging a white sheet over your puppet stage. Shine a flashlight from behind the stage. The people watching will see the shadows of your puppets.

Cat and Dog Boxes

You Will Need:
- **Tagboard**
- **Large empty matchbox**
- **Pen**
- **Paint**
- **Tacky glue**

1 On the tagboard, trace the shape of the matchbox three times. Cut out a square from the first and third shapes. Cut out the whole shape. Glue this shape to the back of some stamped felt (see page 4). With a pen, scratch fold lines on the paper. Cut off the felt around the edges.

2 Fold the shape around the matchbox and glue it in place.

3 Make the head and the tail by gluing felt to tagboard. Cut small pieces of felt for the eyes, nose, and the inside of the ears. Glue these details to the head.

4 Glue the head to the front of the box and the tail to the back.

Cats and dogs cannot see color as well as humans can. Both cats and dogs see most things in shades of gray. But cats and dogs can see even the smallest movement.

29

patterns

Trace the design onto
some tracing paper.
Cut out the pattern.
Pin it to a piece of felt.
Cut the felt following
the pattern.

30

31

index